BACKYARD BIRDS

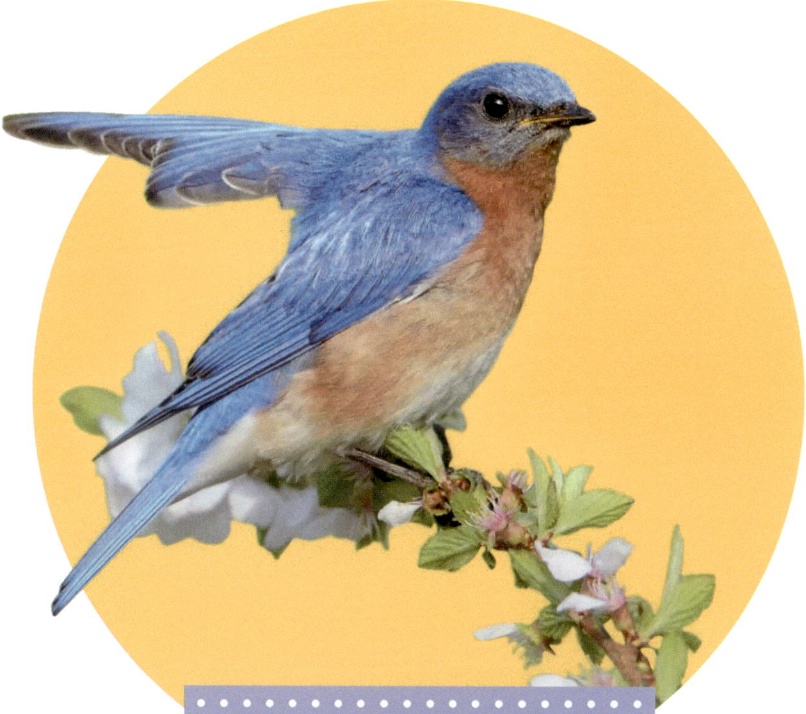

BLUEBIRDS

by Anastasia Suen

beak

nest box

Look for these words and pictures as you read.

eggs

mealworms

Have you seen this bird?
It may be in your yard.
A bluebird has blue feathers.

Chirp! Chirp!
A bluebird is a songbird.
It has a pointed beak.

nest box

Bluebirds make a nest.
They build it in a nest box.
They use grass and weeds.

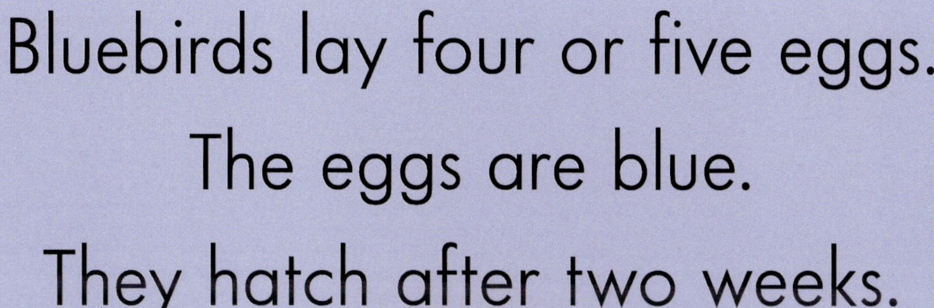

Bluebirds lay four or five eggs.
The eggs are blue.
They hatch after two weeks.

eggs

Bluebirds come to feeders.
They eat mealworms.
They eat bugs and berries.

Splish! Splash!
Bluebirds like water.
A birdbath washes
the dust away.

A bluebird is a backyard bird. Have you seen it?

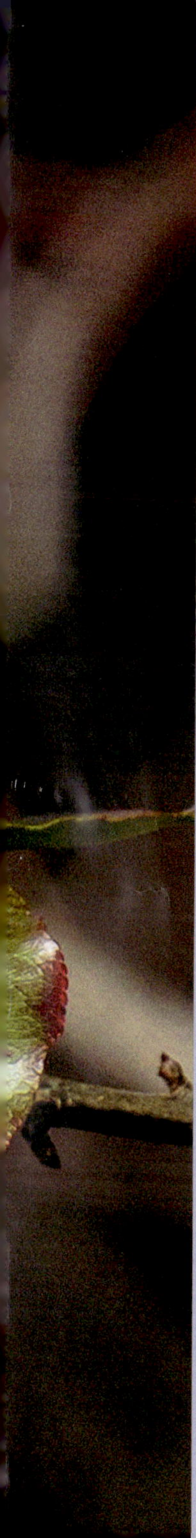

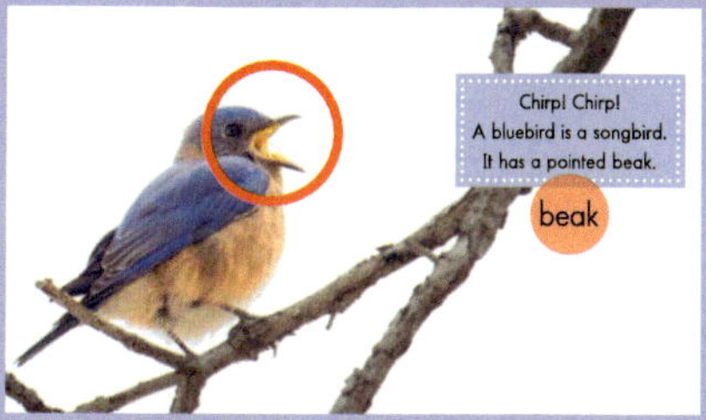
Chirp! Chirp!
A bluebird is a songbird.
It has a pointed beak.
beak

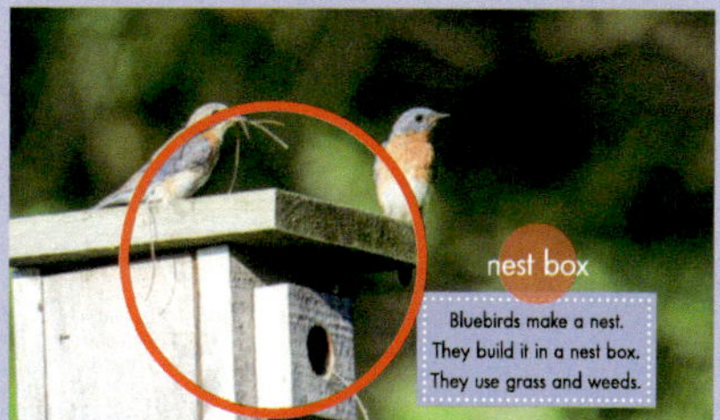

beak

nest box
Bluebirds make a nest.
They build it in a nest box.
They use grass and weeds.

nest box

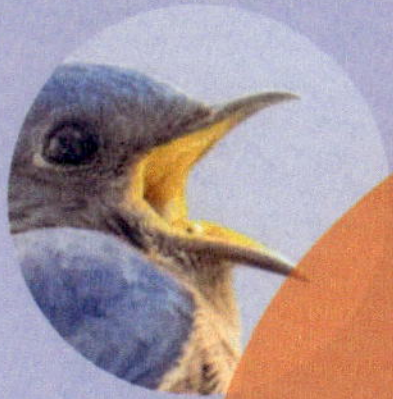

Did you find?

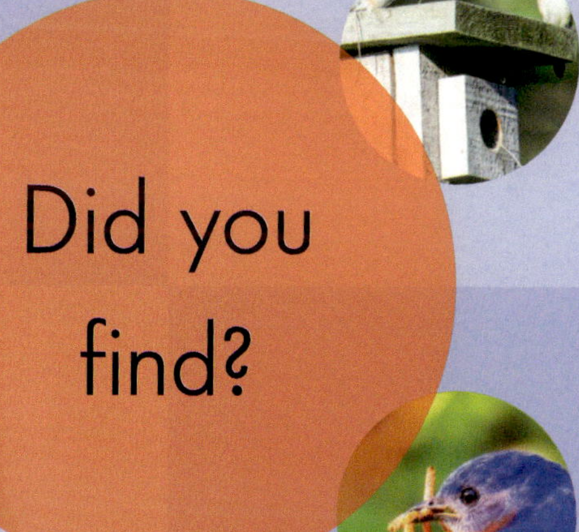

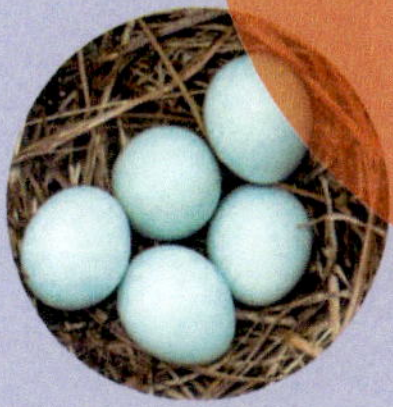

eggs

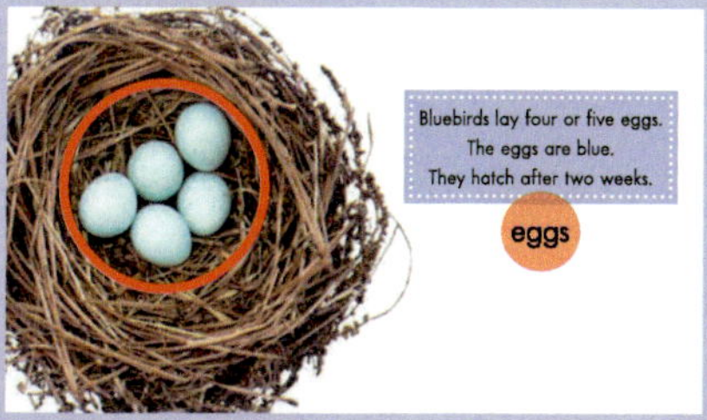
Bluebirds lay four or five eggs.
The eggs are blue.
They hatch after two weeks.
eggs

mealworms

mealworms
Bluebirds come to feeders.
They eat mealworms.
They eat bugs and berries.

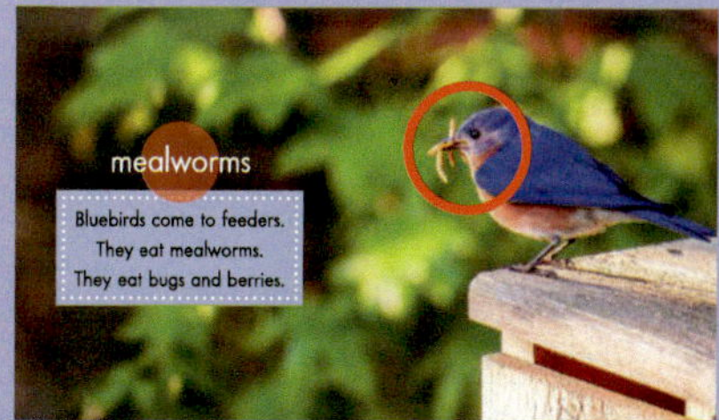

Spot is published by Amicus Learning, an imprint of Amicus
P.O. Box 227, Mankato, MN 56002
www.amicuspublishing.us

Library of Congress Cataloging-in-Publication Data
Names: Suen, Anastasia author
Title: Bluebirds / by Anastasia Suen.
Description: Mankato, MN : Amicus Learning, an imprint of Amicus, [2026] | Series: Spot backyard birds | Audience: Ages 4–7 | Audience: Grades K–1 | Summary: "Bluebirds are small birds with blue feathers found across North America. This search-and-find book reinforces new vocabulary words with simple facts and compelling photographs to teach kindergarten and first grade readers about backyard birds"– Provided by publisher.
Identifiers: LCCN 2025010588 (print) | LCCN 2025010589 (ebook) | ISBN 9798892008297 library binding | ISBN 9798892008952 paperback | ISBN 9798892009614 ebook
Subjects: LCSH: Bluebirds—Juvenile literature
Classification: LCC QL696.P288 S84 2026 (print) | LCC QL696.P288 (ebook) | DDC 598.8/42—dc23/eng/20250721
LC record available at https://lccn.loc.gov/2025010588
LC ebook record available at https://lccn.loc.gov/2025010589

Printed in United States of America

Ana Brauer, editor
Deb Miner, series designer
Sara Hood, book designer and photo researcher

Photos by Getty Images/Gary W. Carter, 3, Josh Atkinson / 500px, 14; Shutterstock/Agnieszka Bacal, 1, Bonnie Taylor Barry, 2, 8–9, 15, 12–13, Chris Hill, 2, 6–7, 15, Dee Carpenter Originals, 2, 4–5, 15, Ilana Block, cover, 16, Wileydoc, 2, 10–11, 15